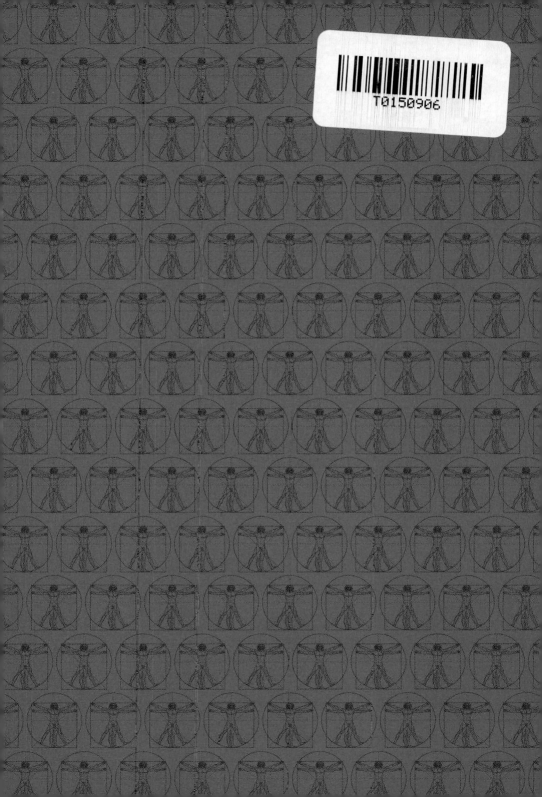

BIOGRAPHIC
LEONARDO

BIOGRAPHIC
LEONARDO

ANDREW KIRK

AMMONITE
PRESS

First published 2017 by
Ammonite Press
an imprint of Guild of Master Craftsman Publications Ltd
Castle Place, 166 High Street, Lewes, East Sussex, BN7 1XU,
United Kingdom

Text © Andrew Kirk, 2017
Copyright in the Work © GMC Publications Ltd, 2017

ISBN 978 1 78145 290 5

A catalogue record for this book is available from the
British Library.

Publisher: Jason Hook
Concept Design: Matt Carr
Design & Illustration: Matt Carr & Robin Shields
Editor: Jamie Pumfrey
Consultant Editor: Dr Grant Pooke
Picture Research: Hedda Roennevig

Colour reproduction by GMC Reprographics
Printed and bound in China

CONTENTS

ICONOGRAPHIC   06

INTRODUCTION   08

01: LIFE   11

02: WORLD   35

03: WORK   51

04: LEGACY   77

BIOGRAPHIES   92

INDEX   94

ACKNOWLEDGMENTS   96

ICONOGRAPHIC

WHEN WE CAN RECOGNIZE AN ARTIST BY
A SET OF ICONS, WE CAN ALSO RECOGNIZE
HOW COMPLETELY THAT ARTIST AND THEIR
WORK HAVE ENTERED OUR CULTURE
AND OUR CONSCIOUSNESS.

INTRODUCTION

Leonardo da Vinci. Genius. Polymath. The archetypal Renaissance man. Painter, draughtsman, architect, inventor, anatomist, mathematician, botanist, geologist, cartographer, civil engineer, mechanical engineer, military engineer – the list of accomplishments trips off the tongue so readily that it is difficult to take in the scope of Leonardo's endeavours.

Worse, perhaps we begin to think that he is too good to be true. There is no grand statement such as the ceiling of the Sistine chapel, painted with such anguish and devotion over so many years by his rival Michelangelo, nothing that shouts "si monumentum requiris, circumspice". Instead there is the *Mona Lisa*, a small portrait marooned in splendid isolation in its room in the Louvre, impossible to see properly as potential admirers are swept past its bulletproof glass enclosure on a tide of tourists with selfie sticks. Copied, parodied, borrowed to add a veneer of enigma to the covers of clunky blockbuster novels, perhaps the *Mona Lisa* is, like its creator, a victim of its own success.

"BEYOND A BEAUTY OF BODY NEVER TO BE SUFFICIENTLY EXTOLLED, THERE WAS AN ENDLESS GRACE IN ALL HIS ACTIONS; AND SO GREAT AND OF SUCH A KIND WAS HIS GENIUS, THAT TO WHATEVER DIFFICULT THINGS HE TURNED HIS MIND, HE SOLVED THEM WITH EASE."

—Giorgio Vasari, *Lives of the Painters*, 1550

To get some perspective, it's best to leave the Louvre and go to Windsor Castle to look at Leonardo's anatomical drawings. One of these explores the workings of the heart, probably the heart of an ox, which Leonardo had dissected so as to reproduce its structures in some detail. Below the aortic valve he observed a swelling, known as the sinus of Valsava, which he injected with wax. He then removed the organic material from around the wax and used the cast to make a glass model of the structure. By pumping water mixed with grass seeds through the model, he was able to observe and draw the vortices that were created, and concluded that these vortices must play a significant role in the operation of the aortic valve. It was not until the middle of the twentieth century that Leonardo's speculations were confirmed by cardiologists. These tiny drawings are on one page of about 600 that came into the collection of the British Royal Family around 1690, and they show that, far from being a painter who dabbled in other things, Leonardo was an experimental scientist of immense sophistication.

Leonardo's anatomical studies were never published in his lifetime, and nor were any of his other projected treatises on art, hydraulics or geometry. This is perhaps in part why the myth of Leonardo has become so powerful, because his achievements are so diffuse and unwieldy, collected in fragmentary notebooks in museums all over the world.

Leonardo will not fit neatly into any category but instead leaps beyond all our efforts to define him. All the lists of inventions, the pages of drawings, the reconstructions of lost works somehow defy our comprehension. In the end, like the *Mona Lisa*, he is just there, clearly rooted in the context of fifteenth-century Italy, yet somehow also inescapably part of our modern world.

"THE MEN OF EXPERIMENT ARE LIKE THE ANT; THEY ONLY COLLECT AND USE. BUT THE BEE GATHERS ITS MATERIALS FROM THE FLOWERS OF THE GARDEN AND OF THE FIELD, BUT TRANSFORMS AND DIGESTS IT BY A POWER OF ITS OWN."

—Leonardo, *Notebooks*, c. 1510

LEONARDO DA VINCI

01
LIFE

"THE ABBREVIATORS OF WORKS DO INJURY TO KNOWLEDGE AND TO LOVE, FOR LOVE OF ANYTHING IS THE OFFSPRING OF KNOWLEDGE, LOVE BEING MORE FERVENT AS KNOWLEDGE IS MORE CERTAIN, AND CERTAINTY SPRINGS FROM A THOROUGH KNOWLEDGE OF ALL THOSE PARTS WHICH COMPOSE THE WHOLE ..."

—Leonardo, *Notebooks*, c. 1510

LEONARDO DI SER PIERO DA VINCI

was born at 10.30pm on 15 April 1452 in the Tuscan hill town of Vinci

Leonardo was the illegitimate son of Ser Piero da Vinci, a lawyer, and Caterina, a farmer's daughter about whom little else is known. Leonardo probably spent most of his childhood in Vinci, where – as the son of a successful professional – he would have received a good basic education. His later well-documented struggles with Latin suggest that his schooling might have been limited to what would be required for a commercial, rather than an artistic or literary, career. Ser Piero had established a successful practice in Florence during the 1450s and 1460s before obtaining an official civil service position with the Medici administration. So when the time came for Leonardo to start making his way in the world, it was natural that he would move to Florence, where his father was able to make the necessary introductions to get him established.

◀ Also born in Tuscany: **Michelangelo Buonarroti** (1475–1564), sculptor and painter and Leonardo's great rival

TUSCANY

VINCI

ITALY

Ludovico Sforza, the future Duke of Milan and Leonardo's patron, is born on 27 July.

THE WORLD IN 1452

MURCIA

The combined forces of the Kingdoms of Castille and Murcia defeat the Moors at the Battle of Los Alporchones.

Leonardo was born at the start of the Early Modern era, the period that followed the Late Middle Ages. It was a time of social and cultural change and achievement, and marked the beginning of globalization as Europeans explored and colonized other parts of the world. The fall of Constantinople to the Ottoman Turks in 1453 and the movements that led to the Protestant Reformation challenged traditional views about Christianity. Newly established trade routes would eventually lead to global mapping, and the invention of Gutenberg's printing press played a part in the wider dissemination of new ideas and discoveries. During this period, Florence would become a hub for artistic, technological and scientific progress, the perfect time for Leonardo to enter the picture.

FLORENCE

Lorenzo Ghiberti completes the bronze doors of the Florence Baptistery, known as the *Gates of Paradise*.

NORTHAMPTONSHIRE

Richard Plantagenet, the future Richard III of England, is born on 2 October in Fotheringhay Castle.

ROME

Frederick III is crowned Holy Roman Emperor on 19 March; he is the last to be crowned by a pope in Rome.

VANUATU

An eruption of the South Pacific volcano Kuwae, in Vanuatu, releases huge amounts of sulphates and causes global cooling.

Antonio da Vinci
(Grandfather)

Lucia da Vinci
(Grandmother)

Francesco di
Antonio da Vinci
(Uncle - Died 1507)

Ser Piero di
Antonio da Vinci
(Father 1427-1504)

Caterina
(Mother)

Leonardo di Ser
Piero da Vinci
(1452-1519)

LEONARDO'S FAMILY TREE

As a child Leonardo was looked after by his grandfather, Antonio, and his stepmother, Albiera, and he was listed as a dependant in his grandfather's tax return in 1457. He was also cared for by his uncle, Francesco, a relationship that must have remained close since Francesco made Leonardo his sole heir on his death in 1507.

2nd Wife
married 1465
Francesca di Ser Giuliano Lanfredini

4th Wife
Lucrezia di Guglielmo Cortigiani
(Died after 1520)

1st Wife
married 1453
Albiera di Giovanni Amadori
(Died 1464)

3rd Wife
married 1475
Margherita di Francesco
(1458–1486)

6 CHILDREN
Antonio, Giuliano, Lorenzo, Maddalena, Violante, Domenico

6 CHILDREN
Margherita, Benedetto, Pandolfo, Guglielmo, Bartolomeo, Giovanni

EARLY LEONARDO

Having spent much of his early life in the natural beauty and relative tranquillity of the Tuscan hills, at 16 Leonardo found himself thrust into the hustle and bustle of city life in Florence. According to Giorgio Vasari, Leonardo had shown early artistic promise and had decorated a shield for a neighbour with a painting of a terrifying monster. As a respected civil servant, his father was in a position to get him apprenticed to one of the most prestigious workshops in the city, where his extraordinary talent began to be trained and developed.

1481

Leonardo leaves Florence for Milan to enter the employment of Ludovico Sforza, the Duke of Milan.

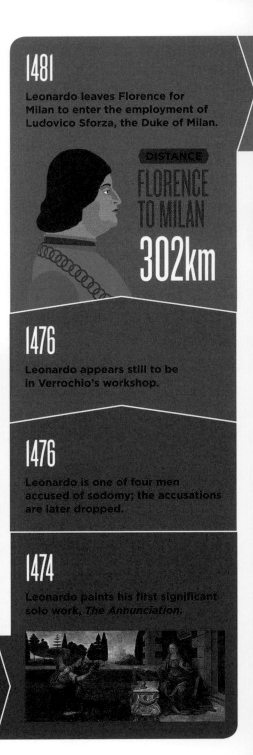

DISTANCE

FLORENCE TO MILAN

302km

1476

Leonardo appears still to be in Verrochio's workshop.

1476

Leonardo is one of four men accused of sodomy; the accusations are later dropped.

1474

Leonardo paints his first significant solo work, *The Annunciation*.

c. 1469

Leonardo moves to Florence and enters the workshop of Andrea del Verrocchio as a pupil.

1472

Leonardo appears in the account book of the painter's confraternity, the Compagnia di S. Luca, Florence.

1473

Leonardo inscribes his first known extant drawing, a Tuscan landscape, "day of St Mary of the Snow, 5 August 1473".

1482

Ludovico commissions Leonardo to make an equestrian statue, the Sforza horse, a monument to his father, Francesco.

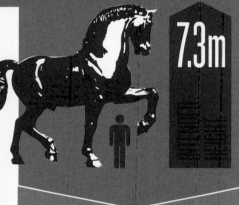

7.3m

1496

King Louis XII of France enters Milan and deposes Ludovico; Leonardo leaves Milan.

1483

Leonardo is commissioned to paint an altarpiece for the chapel of the Confraternity of the Immaculate Conception in the church of S. Francesco il Grande; this eventually results in *The Virgin of the Rocks*.

1495

Leonardo begins work on *The Last Supper* on the wall of the refectory of the convent of Santa Maria della Grazie.

1493

A model of the Sforza horse is displayed in Milan Cathedral during festivities to mark the marriage of Ludovico's niece, Bianca Maria, to the Hapsburg Emperor, Maximilian I.

1494

Ludovico commandeers the bronze for the Sforza horse to make cannons in preparation for a French invasion.

SNAPPY DRESSER

Leonardo was described as handsome by contemporaries, with a well-trimmed beard and lively conversation. He seems also to have had a striking taste in clothes, to judge by a list of garments that he had stored for safekeeping when he went on a military mission in 1504.

I GRAIN-COLOURED HAT

I OVERCOAT OF CRIMSON SATIN, À LA FRANÇAISE

I DARK PURPLE CAPE, WITH BIG COLLAR AND A HOOD OF VELVET

I PAIR OF DUSTY-ROSE TIGHTS

I PAIR OF DARK PURPLE TIGHTS

PLUS: I SHIRT OF REIMS LINEN, WORKED À LA FRANÇAISE

2 PINK CAPS

"THE PAINTER SITS IN FRONT OF HIS WORK WELL DRESSED AND MOVES A VERY LIGHT BRUSH WITH LOVELY COLOURS, AND IS ADORNED WITH CLOTHES AS HE PLEASES ..."

—Leonardo, *Treatise on Painting*

1 PINK CATALAN GOWN

PLUS: 1 DARK PURPLE CAMEL-HAIR OVERCOAT, 1 GOWN OF TAFFETA, 1 PAIR OF BLACK TIGHTS, 1 ARAB CLOAK

1 LINING OF VELVET THAT CAN BE USED AS A GOWN

THE LEFT HAND OF GENIUS?

Apart from knowing that he painted the *Mona Lisa*, the other thing that most people know about Leonardo is that he was left-handed, like all artistic geniuses. This is attested by numerous contemporary witnesses, as well as by the use of mirror-writing in his notebooks – easier to do if you are a leftie. Sadly for the left-handed genius theory, however there is evidence (and in some cases definitive proof) that some of the other painters who routinely appear in lists of left-handed artists were not so.

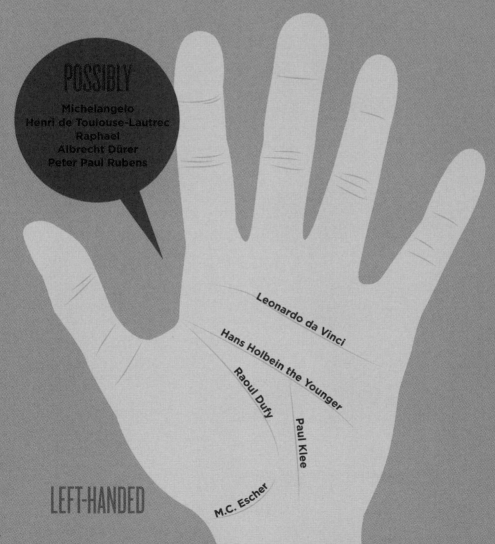

POSSIBLY

Michelangelo
Henri de Toulouse-Lautrec
Raphael
Albrecht Dürer
Peter Paul Rubens

Leonardo da Vinci
Hans Holbein the Younger
Raoul Dufy
Paul Klee
M.C. Escher

LEFT-HANDED

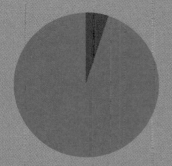

Proportion of left-handed artists: 3–5%*

Proportion of left-handers in the general Western population: 12–14%*

*According to the *Revue Neurologique* 1995

Vincent van Gogh

Pablo Picasso

Rembrandt

Edvard Munch

Claude Monet

RIGHT-HANDED

VEGETARIAN MAN

Vegetarianism was advocated and practised by various Classical thinkers, including Pythagoras, Empedocles and Plotinus. The general revival of interest in the classical world that underlay the Renaissance included the rediscovery of vegetarianism, which had ceased to be practised with the arrival of Christianity. Leonardo's conviction that all aspects of the natural world were interconnected led him to adopt a vegetarian diet as well. His notebooks include shopping lists of herbs and pulses, as well as recipes, including one that seems to be his patent herb sauce.

LEONARDO

HERB SAUCE

"MAN AND THE ANIMALS ARE PROPERLY THE TRANSIT AND CONDUIT OF FOOD, THE SEPULCHRE OF ANIMALS AND THE HOTEL OF THE DEAD."

—Leonardo, *Notebooks*, c. 1510

Porphyry of Tyre (c. 234–c. 305) wrote the first known treatise in favour of vegetarianism, *On Abstinence from Beings with a Soul*

1

Take half a pint of vinegar and heat gently.

2

Roughly chop one handful each of parsley, mint and wild thyme.

LEONARDO'S HERB SAUCE

- half pint of vinegar

- handful of parsley

- handful of mint

- handful of wild thyme

- handful of burnt breadcrumbs

- pinch of salt

- pinch of pepper

3

Pour the warmed vinegar into a jar and add the herbs. Allow to infuse overnight.

5

Reheat the mixture, season with salt and pepper and serve warm.

4

Add one handful of burnt bread, ground into crumbs.

LEONARDO'S LIBRARY

Leonardo made an inventory of his books for safekeeping in 1504. He listed 116 volumes together with another 50 unnamed books, which was a substantial number at that time. The spread of themes gives an idea of the range of his interests.

40 Scientific and medical subjects

40 Literary works or grammars

12 Religious stories and tracts

10 Art, architecture and engineering

14 Miscellaneous

50 Unnamed

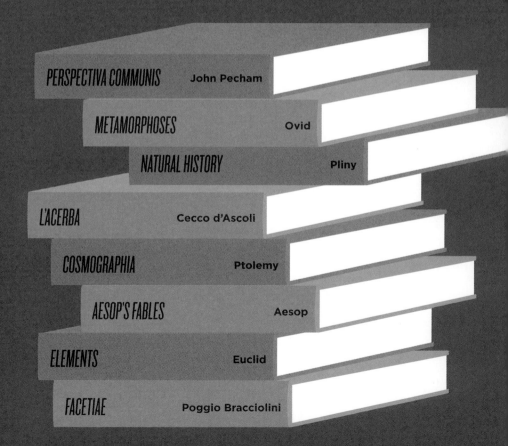

PERSPECTIVA COMMUNIS — John Pecham

METAMORPHOSES — Ovid

NATURAL HISTORY — Pliny

L'ACERBA — Cecco d'Ascoli

COSMOGRAPHIA — Ptolemy

AESOP'S FABLES — Aesop

ELEMENTS — Euclid

FACETIAE — Poggio Bracciolini

VAPRIO D'ADDA

Invading Swiss soldiers set fire to Milan in 1511. Leonardo leaves for the Melzi family villa.

MILAN

At the request of Charles II, the French governor of Milan, Leonardo departs for Milan in 1506, leaving the *Battle of Anghiari* unfinished.

PAVIA

In 1516 Leonardo enters the service of Francis I as court painter.

PISA

Leonardo works on military plans relating to the Florentine siege of Pisa in 1503.

FLORENCE

In 1507 Leonardo records his dissection of a "100 year-old man" at the hospital of Santa Maria Nuova in Florence.

Leonardo is commissioned in 1503 by the Florentine city council to paint a mural depicting the *Battle of Anghiari* in the Great Council Hall.

In 1503 Leonardo begins work on a portrait of Lisa Gherardini, the wife of a silk merchant, Francesco del Giocondo, which will become known as the *Mona Lisa*.

ROMAGNA

In 1502 Leonardo is employed by Cesare Borgia, Captain General of the Papal Armies, as "familiar architect and general engineer".

VENICE

In 1500 Leonardo works for the Venetian Republic on defences against the Turkish threat; in late spring he returns to Florence.

ROME

Leonardo arrives in 1513 as part of the household of Giuliano de' Medici, the brother of Pope Leo X; he has a workshop in the Belvedere palace.

AMBOISE, FRANCE

On 23 April 1519 Leonardo goes before the royal court to acknowledge his will; on 2 May he dies in the Palace of Cloux.

GENIUS FOR HIRE...

In 1499 the Second Italian War broke out and the French invaded Milan, overthrowing Ludovico Sforza and forcing Leonardo, his assistant Salai and friend Luca Pacioli to flee the city. He briefly visited Venice before heading back to Florence, returning as a success. Leonardo's various commissions would then take him across Italy and into France.

LYON, FRANCE

A mechanical lion, invented by Leonardo, is presented as a gift from Lorenzo di Piero de' Medici to Francis I on his return to France from Italy in 1515.

ROMORANTIN, FRANCE

Leonardo works on plans for a palace for the king in 1517.

LEONARDO'S SONS...

Leonardo was known for his entourage of handsome young assistants, whose expenses for clothes and haircuts recur in his accounts. In the absence of a conventional marriage and family, these glamorous boys were Leonardo's alternative household. Of all his pupils, his most long-lasting relationships were with two in particular, Gian Giacomo Caprotti and Francesco Melzi, who were apprenticed to him as children.

GIAN GIACOMO CAPROTTI, KNOWN AS SALAÌ
1480 – 1524

Salaì, the 'little devil', joined Leonardo's household when he was 10, and the notebooks record numerous instances of him stealing cash and property from those around him. Leonardo described him as "thief, liar, obstinate, glutton", but he also spoke of his beautiful curly hair, and Salaì's roguish charm clearly made up for his light fingers.

GIOVANNI FRANCESCO MELZI
c. 1491 – c. 1570

Melzi came from a noble family and joined Leonardo some time before 1510. He became Leonardo's favourite and was instrumental in preserving the precious notebooks after the artist's death.

WAS LEONARDO GAY?

Leonardo's otherwise compendious notebooks reveal very little about his private life, though most authorities agree that he was probably gay. Homosexuality was common in quattrocento Florence and Leonardo was never married. Having escaped a potentially ruinous accusation of sodomy in 1476, perhaps it is not surprising that he was circumspect about this aspect of his personality.

OTHER PUPILS

MARCO D'OGGIONO
c. 1470–1549
Born near Milan, but almost nothing else is known about him. He copied various of Leonardo's works, especially *The Last Supper*.

GIOVANNI BOLTRAFFIO
1466–1516
Born in Milan of an aristocratic family, he was the most accomplished of Leonardo's pupils.

LEONARDO'S DEATH

Leonardo died on 2 May 1519 in the Palace of Cloux at Amboise while in the service of Francis I. He was 67. While the story that he died in the king's arms is fanciful (Francis was miles away at the time), there is little doubt that the French king viewed Leonardo as a valued adornment to his court. His followers were inconsolable, and they duly took up the responsibility of preserving his legacy. Salaì assumed custody of the masterpieces that had accompanied Leonardo on his travels around the courts of Europe while Melzi took charge of the extensive manuscript notebooks.

"IT WOULD BE IMPOSSIBLE FOR ME TO BE ABLE TO EXPRESS THE GRIEF UNDER WHICH I HAVE FALLEN, AND AS LONG AS THE ELEMENTS OF MY BODY REMAIN CONJOINED I WILL BE IN PERPETUAL SADNESS."

—Melzi, letter to Leonardo's half-brother, Lorenzo, 1519

60
beggars followed Leonardo's funeral procession

LEONARDO
DA VINCI

02
WORLD

"THE FIRST METHOD FOR ESTIMATING THE INTELLIGENCE OF A RULER IS TO LOOK AT THE MEN HE HAS AROUND HIM."

—Niccolò Machiavelli, *The Prince*, 1513

CITY STATES

The Italian peninsula at the time of Leonardo was divided into regions, many based around cities that had survived the fall of the Roman Empire and retained Roman republican political institutions. Separated from the rest of Europe by the Alps, these city states were largely autonomous and did not fall under the control of absolute monarchs. The rivalry between these independent republics is often credited as the source of the rapid developments in commerce, finance, urbanization, culture and arts that we now know as the Renaissance.

THE ITALIAN POPULATION DOUBLED BETWEEN THE 11TH AND 14TH CENTURIES

10,000,000

5,000,000

AD1001   AD1301

MORE THAN ONE-THIRD OF THE MALE POPULATION WAS LITERATE IN THE 13TH CENTURY, THE LARGEST PROPORTION IN EUROPE

VENICE, FLORENCE AND MILAN EACH HAD MORE THAN

100,000

INHABITANTS

VENICE

FLORENCE

ROME

20%

OF THE POPULATION LIVED IN CITIES

THE FLORENTINE
LUCA PACIOLI
(c. 1447–1517)

INVENTED MODERN ACCOUNTANCY AND BOOK-KEEPING

1 + 1 = 2

RIVAL CITY STATES

Florence and Milan were the twin epicentres of Leonardo's professional life. Florence was the nurturing ground for his artistic and intellectual development, while Milan provided the environment in which some of his greatest works were conceived and executed.

MILAN/MILANO

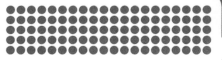

Population: approx. 100,000
● = 1,000

FLORENCE/FIRENZE

GOVERNMENT

A republic ruled by a council of nine but dominated by the Medici family.

ECONOMIC BASIS

Banking and wool.

IMPORTANT BUILDINGS

1. Santa Maria del Fiore 2. Ponte Vecchio 3. Palazzo Vecchio.

NOTABLE FIGURES

Niccolò Machiavelli (1469–1527)
Lorenzo de' Medici (1449–92)
Girolamo Savonarola (1452–98)

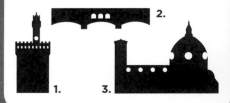

Population: approx. 200,000
● = 1,000

GOVERNMENT
A tyranny under the control of Ludovico Sforza, Duke of Milan.

ECONOMIC BASIS
Trade, silk and agriculture.

NOTABLE FIGURES
Francesco Sforza (1401–66)
Ludovico Sforza (1452–1508)

IMPORTANT BUILDINGS
1. Castello Sforzesco 2. Santa Maria delle Grazie 3. Milan Cathedral

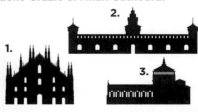

LEONARDO THE DARWINIAN

The Christian tradition held that humans were spiritual beings, somewhere between God and the animals. Leonardo's intense conviction of the interrelatedness of all natural organisms led him to a view that would have been seen as heretical in his day, which was that humans were made of the same stuff as animals, and that all living organisms were connected. In this he anticipated by 350 years the modern picture of the natural world that was established by Charles Darwin.

> "MAN. THE DESCRIPTION OF MAN, WHICH IN IT CONTAINS THAT OF THOSE ANIMALS ALMOST OF LIKE SPECIES, SUCH AS THE BABOON, THE MONKEY AND SUCH LIKE, WHICH ARE MANY."

—Leonardo,
Notebooks,
c. 1510

LINNAEUS

CHARLES DARWIN
(1809–82)

LEONARDO / DARWIN

Charles Darwin published *On the Origin of Species* in 1859. This proposed two key ideas. First, all animal species are descended from common ancestors. Second, the diversity of species has come about from the favouring of specific physical variations that gave a creature a competitive advantage in the struggle to survive and reproduce.

The standard taxonomies, such as that perfected by Carl Linnaeus (1707–78), had humans at the top and other animals ranked below according to their differences from humans. Leonardo and Darwin effectively started from the bottom, with the basic building blocks of animal life.

LEONARDO'S CONNECTIONS

- ● artists
- ● politicians
- ● scientists/engineers

DOMENICO GHIRLANDAIO
(1449–94)
Florentine painter, alongside Leonardo a member of Verrocchio's workshop.

ANDREA DEL VERROCCHIO
(c. 1435–88)
Florentine painter and sculptor to whom Leonardo was apprenticed.

FILIPPINO LIPPI
(1459–1504)
Painter who completed at least two of Leonardo's unfinished commissions.

ANTONIO POLLAIUOLO
(1429–98)
Florentine painter and sculptor, the leader of the rival workshop to Verrocchio's.

GIORGIO VASARI
(1511–74)
Painter and historian who wrote Leonardo's biography and painted over his unfinished *Battle of Anghiari* in the Florentine Council Chamber.

MICHELANGELO
(1475–1564)
Sculptor, painter, architect and Leonardo's great rival.

NICCOLÒ MACHIAVELLI
(1469–1527)

Diplomat and political philosopher who collaborated with Leonardo on a scheme to divert the course of the river Arno during the Florentine war with Pisa.

CESARE BORGIA
(1475–1507)

Nobleman and military commander who hired Leonardo as a military consultant to the papal armies.

FRANCESCO DI GIORGIO
(c. 1439–1501)

Sienese architect and engineer, a contemporary of Leonardo in Milan.

LUCA PACIOLI
(c. 1447–1517)

Florentine mathematician whose book *De divina proportione* was illustrated with drawings by Leonardo.

DONATO BRAMANTE
(1444–1514)

Court architect to Ludovico Sforza and a friend of Leonardo.

RAPHAEL
(1483–1520)

Painter and sculptor, influenced by Leonardo's portraiture.

SANDRO BOTTICELLI
(1445–1510)

Florentine painter and a friend of Leonardo.

MICHELANGELO

The idea that these two artistic superstars were not only alive at the same time but lived in the same limited geographical area and worked for many of the same people is astonishing. The fact that they did not see eye to eye is perhaps less astonishing. Michelangelo seems to have viewed Leonardo as a dilettante and a charlatan, while Leonardo saw his young rival as a coarse upstart. The Renaissance art world was fiercely competitive, since there were a limited number of patrons and commissions to go around, but the rivalry between these two struck contemporaries as especially deep-seated.

37
SCULPTURES

89

10
BUILDINGS

OVER
300
POEMS

7
PAINTINGS

BORN 1475 / DIED 1564

CHARACTER
Uncouth, irascible, solitary

GREATEST WORKS
David, Sistine Chapel ceiling

LEONARDO

ABOUT **6,000** MANUSCRIPT PAGES OF NOTES AND DRAWINGS

20 PAINTINGS

GREATEST WORKS

Mona Lisa, The Last Supper

67

CHARACTER

Elegant, charming, convivial

BORN 1452 / DIED 1519

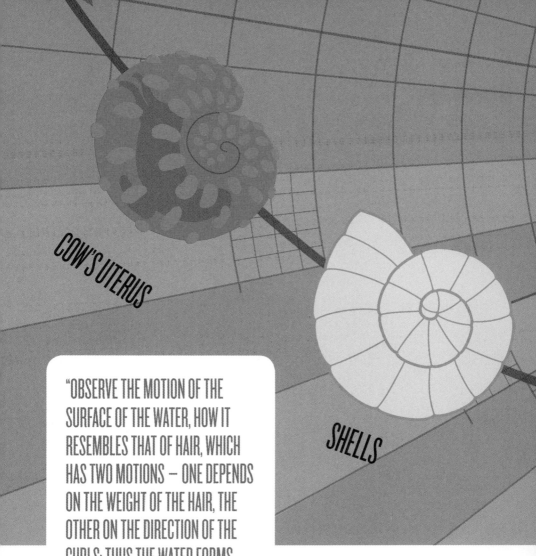

COW'S UTERUS

SHELLS

"OBSERVE THE MOTION OF THE SURFACE OF THE WATER, HOW IT RESEMBLES THAT OF HAIR, WHICH HAS TWO MOTIONS — ONE DEPENDS ON THE WEIGHT OF THE HAIR, THE OTHER ON THE DIRECTION OF THE CURLS; THUS THE WATER FORMS WHIRLING EDDIES, ONE PART FOLLOWING THE IMPETUS OF THE CHIEF CURRENT, AND THE OTHER FOLLOWING THE INCIDENTAL MOTION AND RETURN FLOW."

—Leonardo, *Notebooks*, c. 1510

LEDA'S HAIR

THE VORTEX

Leonardo explored vortices in the flow of air, in the circulation of the blood through the heart, and in the patterns of human hair, as seen in studies for his lost painting *Leda and the Swan*. Vortices were depicted in drawings of shells, plants, a cow's uterus and most dramatically in a series of images of storms. The flow of water was a particular obsession. Leonardo wrote that he had reached "730 conclusions on water" and listed 64 different terms for water in motion.

PARAGONE

The paragone is the term used for an argument that took place intermittently during the Renaissance. They addressed the relative superiority of the different arts in terms of their ability to recreate the forms of nature. Baldassare Castiglione's

The Book of the Courtier includes a debate on the relative merits of painting and sculpture. The debate also served to enhance the status of the visual arts, which had previously been regarded as mere mechanical crafts, unlike poetry and music.

PAINTING IS BEST

- requires imagination as well as technical skill, unlike sculpture

- can represent an entire scene or story

- permits the artist to control colour and light to the best effect

SCULPTURE IS BEST

- is more durable and permanent than painting

- derives directly from the most ancient models and is therefore the primary art form

- allows the depiction of nature in three dimensions

LEONARDO DA VINCI

03
WORK

"THOSE WHO TAKE FOR THEIR GUIDE ANYTHING OTHER THAN NATURE — MISTRESS OF THE MASTERS — EXHAUST THEMSELVES IN VAIN."

—Leonardo, *Notebooks*, c. 1510

THE STUDENT BECOMES THE MASTER

The earliest known example of Leonardo's painting is an angel in the bottom corner of his teacher Verrocchio's *Baptism of Christ*. Compared to Verrocchio's rather angular and static Christ figure, Leonardo's angel glows with an inner vibrancy; the flesh looks warm and soft, and the cascades of golden curls mark him out as a child of Leonardo. The pupil's skill allegedly caused his master to give up painting altogether.

▲ **The Baptism of Christ**
Andrea del Verrocchio
Oil and tempera on wood, 1472–5
70 x 59in (177 x 151cm)

"LEONARDO PAINTED AN ANGEL ... AND DID IT IN SUCH A MANNER THAT THE ANGEL BY LEONARDO WAS MUCH BETTER THAN THE FIGURES BY ANDREA. THIS WAS THE REASON THAT ANDREA NO LONGER WANTED TO TOUCH COLOURS ..."

—**Giorgio Vasari**, *Lives of the Artists*, **1550**

The Annunciation is Leonardo's first-known independent painting. It uses motifs from Verrocchio's studio, but there are elements that indicate Leonardo's mature style.

▲ **The Annunciation**
Oil and tempera on wood, c. 1472–5
38 x 85in (98 x 217cm)

PERSPECTIVE

The painting has a quite mechanical and laborious perspectival scheme, and the Virgin is too far from the lectern, making her arm appear excessively long. It may be that the painting was intended to be viewed from the right.

OBSERVATION

The carpet of flowers and the detail of the rocky landscape in the background show Leonardo's powers of scientific observation.

LIGHT

The suggestion of soft dawn light that gently illuminates the figures is an early indication of the *sfumato*, 'smoky', style that distinguishes his later works, most famously the *Mona Lisa*.

IDEAS TAKE FLIGHT

INSPIRED BY
A BAT'S WING

MADE OF FABRIC
STRETCHED
OVER WOODEN
SKELETON

HELICOPTER
DESIGN

Leonardo returned to the idea of human-powered flight obsessively throughout his career. A whole treatise from 1505, now in Turin, was devoted to studies and drawings of birds and wings, with notes on aerofoil shapes and coefficients of lift. He did make one design for a sort of helicopter, but most of his schemes were for a machine with wings, an *uccello*, a 'bird'. We don't know whether any of his machines were ever tested, though there is a precautionary note next to one of his designs that the test flight should take place over a lake ...

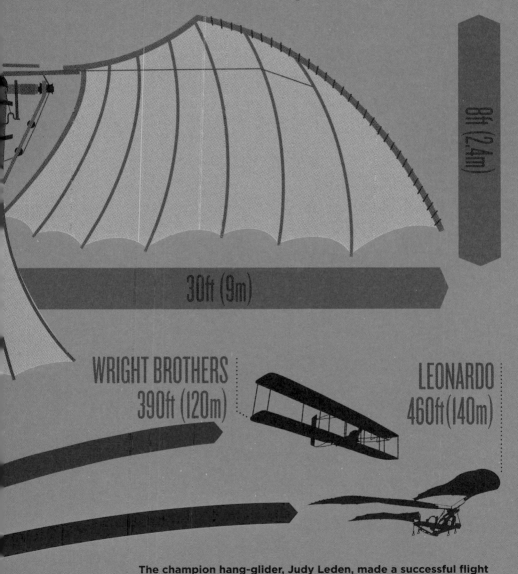

8ft (2.4m)

30ft (9m)

WRIGHT BROTHERS
390ft (120m)

LEONARDO
460ft (140m)

The champion hang-glider, Judy Leden, made a successful flight in 2003 using a glider based on Leonardo's design. The design managed a flight that exceeded the first gliding attempts of the Wright brothers in 1900.

MAY I INTRODUCE...

Leonardo's apparent inability to complete the commissions he received in Florence would suggest that he was ill-suited to the commercial demands put upon the jobbing Renaissance artist. What he needed was a salaried post with a wealthy patron, and Ludovico Sforza, the absolute ruler of the immensely powerful city state of Milan, was the ideal candidate. His letter of introduction shows that Leonardo recognized the priorities of his prospective employer, since he presented himself as primarily a military engineer who dabbled a bit in painting and sculpture.

WHAT IL MAESTRO LEONARDO CAN OFFER ...

01 Portable bridges and "methods of destroying and burning those of the enemy"

02 Draining moats and trenches

03 Methods of ruining every castle and fortress, "even if it is built on rock"

04 Methods of tunnelling

05 Bombards that hurl small stones "almost like a tempest"

06 New types of covered chariots

07 Various kinds of guns of "beautiful and useful forms outside the common usage"

08 Catapults of "marvellous efficacy and outside the common usage"

09 "and if it should occur at sea, I have many types of devices most effective for offence and defence"

AND INCIDENTALLY...

10 "I can carry out sculpture in marble, bronze and clay; similarly in painting also that which can be done to bear comparison with any other ..."

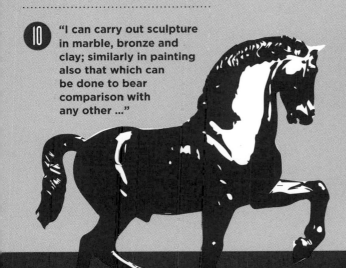

THE CODEX ATLANTICUS

The *Codex Atlanticus* is considered to be the most important collection of Leonardo's drawings and writings in existence. The compendium, which consists of a 12-volume leather-bound set, contains sketches and thoughts on a range of topics from flight and weaponry through to studies in painting and sculpture. Its name derives from its large format, which was comparable to that of an atlas. After his death, Leonardo's pupil, Francesco Melzi, kept all of Leonardo's various writings safely preserved and in one place, but after Melzi's own death the papers were widely dispersed among various art dealers and collectors. In the late 16th century, a large number of

Leonardo's papers were obtained by the Italian sculptor, Pompeo Leoni. He set about mounting the disparate papers on to large sheets, which were used at the time for making atlases, and gradually assembled them into a composite work. The codex eventually found a home at the Biblioteca Ambrosiana in Milan in 1637, where it spent the next 160 years before the French invasion of Italy saw Napoleon Bonaparte transfer the work to the Louvre in Paris in 1796. It was returned to Milan in 1815 and is still at the Biblioteca Ambrosiana, where it is kept in a temperature- and humidity-controlled environment.

VOLUMES

12

CREATED

1478 – 1519

PAGES

1,119

DRAWINGS

1,100

SIZE

25 X 17in (65 X 44cm)

MEDIUM

PEN & INK ON PAPER

Cannons and cannonballs ▼
Codex Atlanticus f. 31 recto.

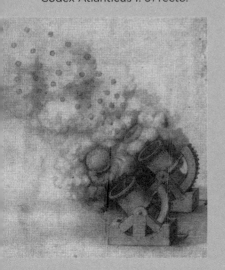

1478–1519

Leonardo creates the *Codex Atlanticus*.

1519

Papers are inherited by Francesco Melzi on Leonardo's death.

1570

Melzi dies, the folios are passed on and ultimately sold.

LATE 1500s

Sculptor Pompeo Leoni assembles the papers into the codex.

1637

Leoni's relatives sell the codex to Marquis Galaezzo Arconati, who donates it to the Biblioteca Ambrosiana.

1796

Napoleon conquers Milan and orders the work to be sent to the Louvre in Paris.

1815

The codex is returned to the Biblioteca Ambrosiana in Milan.

VITRUVIAN MAN

Leonardo's *Vitruvian Man* was a visual expression of the idea of the divine harmony of nature, which had been created by God according to an ideal set of principles and proportions. The archetypal human being was a reflection in miniature of this divine geometry. By extension, the works of architects should also have their basis in the proportions of the human body. The thinkers of the Renaissance systematized this general notion through precise and detailed analyses of perspective and harmonic geometrical relationships.

WHO IS THE *VITRUVIAN MAN*?

The *Vitruvian Man* is a visual representation of a passage in the third book of Vitruvius's *De architectura*, in which the measurements of a perfectly proportioned man are described.

SQUARING THE CIRCLE

'Squaring the Circle' is a famous geometric challenge to construct a circle and square with an equal area. Having thwarted mathematicians and philosophers for centuries, in 1882 it was proven to be impossible, and so the term is more commonly used as a metaphor for trying to do the impossible.

The *Vitruvian Man* fits perfectly into both a circle and a square, and demonstrates that the ideal human proportions correspond to the two ideal geometric figures on which classical architecture is based.

Vitruvius (c. 75 BC–c. 15 BC) was a Roman architect and civil engineer whose 10-volume *De architectura* was hugely influential during the Renaissance.

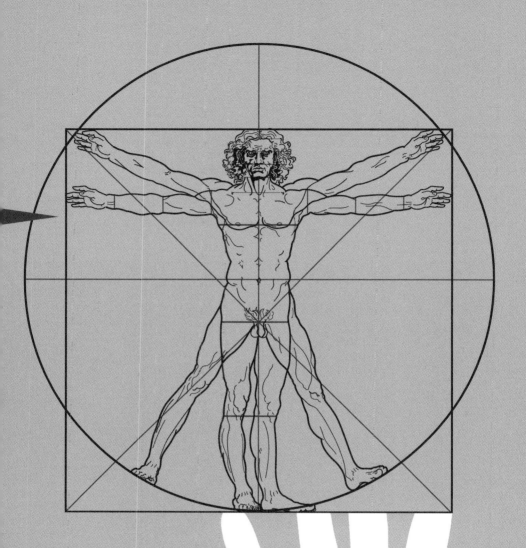

SURROUNDING THE DRAWING IS AN INSCRIPTION, IN LEONARDO'S FAMOUS MIRROR WRITING, THAT READS:

- *a palm is four fingers*
- *a foot is four palms*
- *a cubit is six palms*
- *four cubits make a man*
- *a pace is four cubits*
- *a man is 24 palms*

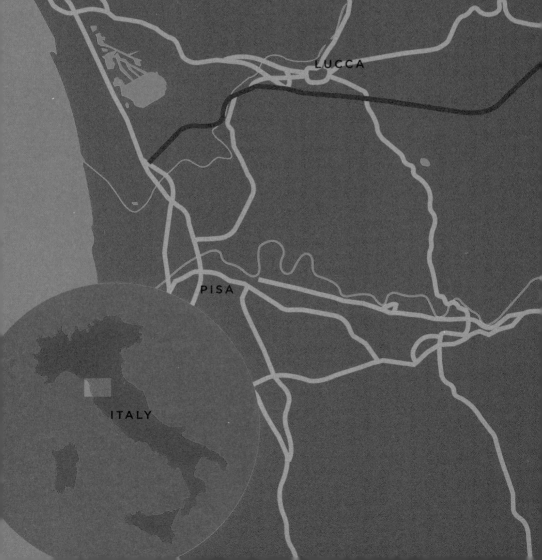

THE CIVIL ENGINEER

In 1504 Leonardo revived an old scheme for a canal from Florence to the navigable section of the Arno west of Pisa, to bypass the rocky meanders that made the river impassable. The map that he produced is a vivid representation of the topography of the area – you can almost hear the rushing water! But Leonardo married sound surveying to his draughtsmanship. His chosen route arced northward across the plains before going through a cutting in the mountains at Serravalle – precisely the route taken by the engineers of the A11 autostrada 400 years later.

LUCCA

PISA

ITALY

**A11
AUTOSTRADA
ROUTE**

SERRAVALLE

FLORENCE

RIVER ARNO

**Geographic ▶
chart of
proposed
canal route**
Drawing with
feather and ink
on black stone,
1503–1504,
Windsor Castle,
Royal Library.

WORK

THE GIANT HORSE

KEY

Equestrian statue
of Gattamelata,
Donatello (1453)

12ft (3.7m) HIGH

Equestrian statue
of Bartolomeo Colleoni,
Andrea del Verrocchio (1488)

13ft (4m) HIGH

Equestrian statue
of Marcus Aurelius
(AD 175)

14ft (4.3m) HIGH

One of Leonardo's first commissions for Ludovico Sforza was to create an equestrian statue of the founder of the Sforza dynasty, his father Francesco. To reflect the status of the Milanese dukedom (and perhaps to extinguish once and for all the ignoble fact that the progenitor of the house of Sforza was an illegitimate mercenary soldier), the monument was projected on an unprecedented scale. Leonardo spent months in the duke's stables making detailed anatomical sketches, and devised the machinery necessary to cast the bronze statue in one piece. The mighty horse (at some point the figure of the rider Francesco seems to have disappeared) took on legendary status, and sadly that was how things stayed, since the French threw Ludovico out of Milan in 1499 and the monument was never completed.

Leonardo's equestrian monument was finally realized in 1999 when a full-size cast was unveiled in Milan. A second cast was commissioned by philanthropist Frederik Meijer and situated in the Frederik Meijer Gardens and Sculpture Park in Grand Rapids, Michigan, also in 1999.

HEIGHT

25ft
(7.6m)

WEIGHT
70 TONS

LIKE A VIRGIN

Leonardo was commissioned by the Confraternity of the Immaculate Conception of the Virgin in Milan to paint an altarpiece for their chapel in the church of S. Francesco il Grande in April 1483. Twenty-five years later, after a saga involving contractual disputes, legal threats, judicial arbitration and the mysterious disappearance of the first version of the *Virgin of the Rocks*, Leonardo's second version was finally in place in the Confraternity's chapel. The story of the two versions reveals the rocky road of working with a genius.

The contrast of light and shade is more pronounced.

The three human figures are lacking haloes.

The botanical drawings are more accurate.

The angel points directly at John the Baptist.

▲ *Virgin of the Rocks* (Paris) **VERSION 1** Oil on wood panel transferred to canvas, 1483–c. 1486 78 x 48in (199 x 122cm)

The landscape is idealized.

The recession of the landscape background is more gradual.

▲ *Virgin of the Rocks* (London) **VERSION 2**
Oil on wood panel,
c. 1495–1508
74 x 47in
(189 x 120cm)

All the figures are slightly bigger.

The colour tone is more uniform.

1483 Leonardo is commissioned to produce an altarpiece for the Confraternity of the Immaculate Conception.

c. 1486 The painting, *Virgin of the Rocks*, is complete but not in place owing to a contract dispute.

1491 Leonardo writes a letter of complaint to Ludovico Sforza about non-payment by the Confraternity for his work.

c. 1493 VERSION 1 is sold, possibly to Ludovico Sforza himself.

c. 1495 VERSION 2 of the painting is begun.

1503 Notaries for the Confraternity draw up a summary of the ongoing payment dispute.

1506 Arbitrators are appointed to negotiate an agreement, and examine the half-finished VERSION 2.

1508 Final payment is received for the completed VERSION 2.

1576 VERSION 2 is removed when the church is demolished.

1625 VERSION 1 is in the French Royal Collection.

1785 VERSION 2 is sold by the Confraternity to the British painter Gavin Hamilton.

1880 VERSION 2 is sold to the National Gallery, London.

WORK

BATTLE OF THE BATTLES

The opportunity for an artistic showdown between Michelangelo and Leonardo came in 1503/4 when each was commissioned by the ruling council of the Florentine Republic to paint a battle scene for their Great Council Chamber. As we can see, the two proposed works exemplify the distinctive passions and preoccupations of the rival artists. In the event, neither work was completed. Michelangelo was called to Rome in 1505 by Pope Julius II to design the pontiff's tomb. Leonardo was required by the French rulers of Milan in 1506, and despite the efforts of the Florentine council to get him to fulfil his contract he never returned to the painting. In 1512 the Spanish sacked Florence and returned the Medici to power, and the great competition was at an end.

MICHELANGELO
BATTLE OF CASCINA

A heroic account of virtuous citizenry arming to defend their city.

Displays Michelangelo's fascination with the nude male body in *contrapposto*.

Indicates a belief in civic virtue and idealism.

▲ *The Battle of Casina* (after Michelangelo)
Copy by Michelangelo's pupil Arisotle de Sangallo
Oil on wood, c. 1542
30 x 51in (77 x 130cm)

The Battle of Anghiari (after Leonardo) ▲
Copy by Peter Paul Rubens
Drawing of the cartoon, c. 1603
18 x 25in (45 x 64cm)

A graphic portrayal
of the savagery of war.

Shows Leonardo's
meticulous attention
to anatomical detail.

Suggests a degree
of scepticism about
heroic and valorous
notions of war.

LEONARDO
BATTLE OF ANGHIARI

Although Michelangelo
never set brush to plaster,
Leonardo did complete part of his
painting, but all efforts to discover
its remains under the subsequent
decoration of the walls by Vasari
have been unsuccessful.

ANATOMY

Leonardo performed dozens of dissections of both humans and animals, including one dissection of a complete human body in the winter of 1507. The accuracy and vitality of his anatomical drawings is unsurpassed, but alongside a 'modern' scientific investigative approach, Leonardo retained the medieval cosmological idea that all of nature follows the same pattern. Human beings were made up of the same elements as the rest of the universe, and so analogies could be seen everywhere.

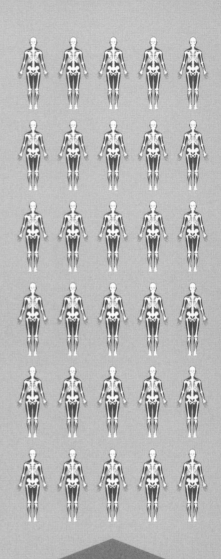

ANATOMICAL MANUSCRIPT A

18 double-sided pages

240+ meticulous drawings

13,000 words

written in "mirror-script"

The collection of studies of the human body made by Leonardo in 1510/11 is kept in the Royal Collection, Windsor. It is known as Anatomical Manuscript A.

30+
CADAVERS DISSECTED
AVERAGING 2 A YEAR

SKULL
Leonardo injected molten wax into a skull to locate the cavities of the cranium and was able to successfully produce accurate anatomical drawings.

BRAIN
In search of the human soul, Leonardo deduced the brain was the body's "command centre".

TORSO
Leonardo produced accurate observations of the placement of organs.

HEART
Leonardo filled a heart with wax and made a plaster cast of it. He identified 4 chambers of the heart, previously thought of as having 2, and suggested, correctly, that arteries fur over a lifetime causing health problems.

LIVER
He drew an oversized liver and correctly identified the cause of death as liver disease.

SPINE
Leonardo's knowledge of engineering was probably a factor in accurately depicting the curvature of the spine and details of vertebrae. However, he incorrectly thought that the spine was the source of semen.

REPRODUCTIVE SYSTEM
Leonardo found difficulty in illustrating the female reproductive system, possibly due to a lack of female cadavers, and his drawings show a system closer to that of a cow.

BIOGRAPHIC THE LAST SUPPER

In 1495 Leonardo was commissioned to paint a mural of *The Last Supper* on the wall of the refectory of the Convent of Santa Maria delle Grazie in Milan. Instead of using the technique of fresco, painting onto wet plaster which absorbs the paint so that it becomes part of the wall,

Leonardo painted on the dry wall using oil and tempera. This allowed him to work slowly to create his characteristic *sfumato* effect, but it proved ruinous for the painting, which began to fall off the wall because of the humid conditions almost as soon as it was finished.

▲ **The Last Supper**
Oil and tempera on plaster, 1495–98
181 x 346in (460 x 880cm)

THE POWER OF THREE

The Last Supper has several references to the Trinity

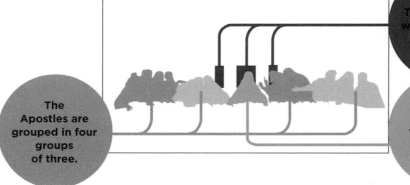

The Apostles are grouped in four groups of three.

There are three windows behind Jesus.

The posture of Jesus with his arms outstretched creates a triangle.

RESTORATIONS

7
attempted
restorations

21
years spent on a
final attempt at
restoration

50,000
hours spent on
the restoration
in total

42%
of the original
painting remains

A HISTORY OF DISASTERS

1400s
1495 Painting commissioned.
1495–98 Painted by Leonardo.

1500s
1517 The painting begins to flake.
1556 Giorgio Vasari describes the
painting as already "ruined".

1600s
1652 A doorway is cut through
the lower part of the painting.

1700s
1796 Anti-clerical French revolutionary
troops attack the painting with stones.

1800s
1821 An attempt to remove the
painting badly damages the centre.

1900s
1943 The refectory is badly
damaged by Allied bombing during
the Second World War.

LOST WORKS

Leonardo completed relatively few paintings, and some – such as *The Last Supper* and his decoration of the Sala delle Asse in the Sforza Castle in Milan – now only remain in a fragmentary state. We know, from contemporary documents including Giorgio Vasari's *Life*, of other paintings by him that have now disappeared. There are also about a dozen whose attribution is disputed.

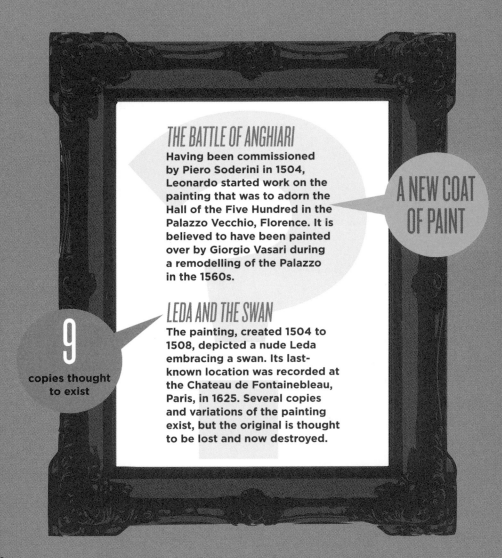

THE BATTLE OF ANGHIARI

Having been commissioned by Piero Soderini in 1504, Leonardo started work on the painting that was to adorn the Hall of the Five Hundred in the Palazzo Vecchio, Florence. It is believed to have been painted over by Giorgio Vasari during a remodelling of the Palazzo in the 1560s.

A NEW COAT OF PAINT

LEDA AND THE SWAN

The painting, created 1504 to 1508, depicted a nude Leda embracing a swan. Its last-known location was recorded at the Chateau de Fontainebleau, Paris, in 1625. Several copies and variations of the painting exist, but the original is thought to be lost and now destroyed.

9
copies thought to exist

LEONARDO DA VINCI

04
LEGACY

"THERE MAY NOT BE IN THE WORLD AN EXAMPLE OF ANOTHER GENIUS SO UNIVERSAL, SO INCAPABLE OF FULFILMENT, SO FULL OF YEARNING FOR THE INFINITE, SO NATURALLY REFINED, SO FAR AHEAD OF HIS OWN CENTURY AND THE FOLLOWING CENTURIES."

—Hippolyte Taine, *Voyage en Italie*, 1866

BIOGRAPHIC MONA LISA

The most famous painting in the world was one that Leonardo seemed unable to bring himself to part with. It was begun in 1503, possibly as a commission from the subject's husband, Francesco del Giocondo, a Florentine silk merchant. If this was the case, then Francesco was destined to be disappointed in the same way as so many of Leonardo's clients, since the painting was still with the artist and hence undelivered when he died in France 16 years later. There has been speculation that Leonardo had some kind of significant relationship with Lisa that explains his unwillingness to let her image go, but there are plenty of elements in the painting itself to account for his attachment to it.

▲ **Mona Lisa**
Oil on wood panel, 1517
30 x 21in (77 x 53cm)

THE GAZE

This is the only one of Leonardo's portraits in which the subject looks directly out of the canvas, creating a degree of psychological intimacy between the work and the viewer that is unprecedented.

THE SMILE

According to Dante, the eyes and the lips were the windows to the soul. Leonardo's portrait exemplifies this perfectly, and brilliantly exploits our instinctive desire to read a person's character through their face. Why is she smiling at us? Or, more pertinently, why is she smiling at me?

THE WATER

More than merely the background, the imagined Tuscan landscape expresses Leonardo's sense of the fundamental patterning of the natural world of which humans are a part. The flowing water is reflected in the waves and rivulets of Lisa's clothes and hair, the spiraling effect of her scarf. The human and the natural dissolve into one another.

MATERIALS

The *Mona Lisa* is an oil painting on a poplar panel. Leonardo used a technique known as *sfumato* to blend colours and he painted with such subtlety that there are no visible brush marks.

Mona Lisa
30 x 21in
(77 x 52cm)

NOT AS BIG AS YOU THINK

Leonardo
5ft 8in
(173cm) tall

15sec
average time spent looking at her

$300,000

paid by each of 6 different wealthy Americans for what they thought was the painting, after it was stolen in 1911.

6,000,000

people visit the *Mona Lisa* at the Louvre in Paris each year.

Picasso was a suspect in the theft of the *Mona Lisa* and was brought in for questioning but later released without charge.

14 possible number of years taken to paint

3 different layers painted underneath the current one

500 years old in 2017

Start | 1503 | | | | | | | | | | | | 1517 | Finish

DID THEY WORK?

Such was the breadth of Leonardo's imagination that it is impossible to say definitively how many different machines he designed, and it is also difficult to be certain about whether any of them were actually produced. And while the flying machines and giant crossbows have captured the imagination of succeeding generations, his less spectacular improvements to gears and industrial machines were probably absorbed into the technological fabric of his time.

LENS GRINDER

INGENIOUS BUT PROBABLY UNWORKABLE

CAR

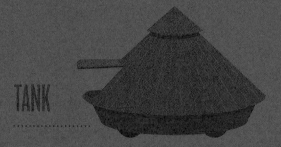

TANK

TESTED SUCCESSFULLY IN THE 20TH CENTURY

SWING BRIDGE

PARACHUTE

BOBBIN-WINDER

WORM GEAR

RACK & PINION

HELICOPTER

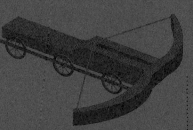

GIANT CROSSBOW

HANG GLIDER

DIVING SUIT

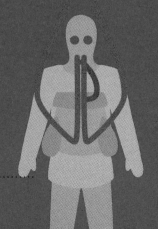

RENAISSANCE MEN (AND WOMEN)

The term 'Renaissance man' was coined in the early 20th century to describe a person with a range of talents and accomplishments, epitomized by the many artists and thinkers in the Renaissance. Leonardo is the epitome of the Renaissance man, but there were others before him and have been others since. There are even (whisper it) Renaissance women …

AL BIRUNI
973–1048

Physicist

Astronomer

Historian

Linguist

Natural scientist

Pharmacologist

HILDEGARD OF BINGEN
1098–1179

Theologian

Poet

Philosopher

Playwright

Composer

Natural historian

Botanist

Physiologist

GALILEO
1564–1642

Astronomer

Engineer

Physicist

Philosopher

Mathematician

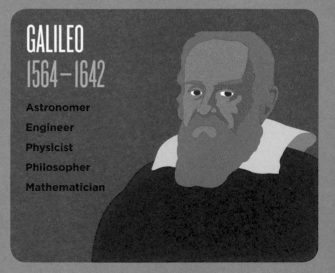

CB FRY
1872–1956

International footballer & cricketer

World long jump record holder

Diplomat

Journalist

Writer

King of Albania (almost)

ORSON WELLES
1915–85

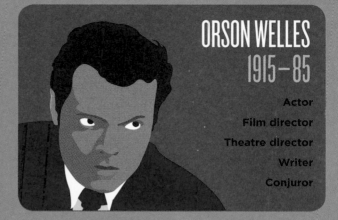

Actor

Film director

Theatre director

Writer

Conjuror

SIMONE DE BEAUVOIR
1908–86

Writer

Intellectual

Philosopher

Political activist

Feminist and social theorist

ALEX COMFORT 1920–2000

Physician

Gerontologist

Sexologist

Marine biologist

Political activist

Poet

Novelist

Psychiatrist

Translator

ADAPTING LEONARDO...

Leonardo's work has been co-opted and adapted in various ways. People have produced working prototypes from his design drawings, other artists have copied and parodied his work, and he has helped at least one blockbuster novel into the bestseller lists. The diverse, suggestive, dense and intensely imagined world he created offers plenty of room for exploration, even 500 years after his death.

THE *MONA LISA* HAS BEEN REPRODUCED USING:

3,000
CUPS OF COFFEE

10,000
JELLY BEANS

5,000
LEGO BRICKS

100,000
GEMSTONES

315
RUBIK'S CUBES

6,000

The Da Vinci Code lists Leonardo as one of the members of the Priory of Sion inserts Mary Magdalene into *The Last Supper*, and has a dead body laid out in the shape of the Vitruvian Man. None of which did any harm to its sales.

Sales of *The Da Vinci Code* approximately:

£82m

Different language editions:

42

FINDING LEONARDO

◀ *A Bear Walking*
Silverpoint on paper, c. 1482–5
4 x 5 in (10 x 13 cm)

▲ *The Virgin and Child with St Anne*
Oil on wood, c. 1503–19
66 x 51in (168 x 130cm)

▲ *St Jerome*
Oil on wood, c. 1482
41 x 29in (103 x 74cm)

PAINTINGS

● **Uffizi Gallery, Florence**
The Annunciation
The Adoration of the Magi

● **Alte Pinakothek, Munich**
The Madonna of the Carnation

● **National Gallery, Washington**
Portrait of Ginevra de' Benci

● **Pinacoteca Vaticana, Rome**
St Jerome Praying in the Wilderness

● **Pinacoteca Ambrosiana, Milan**
Portrait of a Musician

● **Hermitage Museum, St Petersburg**
The Benois Madonna

● **Musée du Louvre, Paris**
Mona Lisa
Virgin of the Rocks
La Belle Ferronnière
The Virgin and Child with St Anne
St John the Baptist

● **Czartoryski Museum, Krakow**
Lady with an Ermine

● **National Gallery, London**
Virgin of the Rocks

● **Santa Maria delle Grazie, Milan**
The Last Supper

● **Private Collection, New York**
Madonna of the Yarnwinder

● **Scottish National Gallery, Edinburgh**
Madonna of the Yarnwinder

NOTEBOOKS

◆ **Biblioteca Ambrosiana, Milan**
Codex Atlanticus (1478–1519)

◆ **Bibliothèque de l'Institut de France, Paris**
Paris Manuscripts A–M
Codex Ashburnham I and *II* (c. 1492)

◆ **Biblioteca Trivulziana, Milan**
Codex Trivulzianus (c. 1487–90)

◆ **Biblioteca Nacional de España, Madrid**
Codex Madrid I (1490s)
Codex Madrid II (1503–04)

◆ **Victoria and Albert Museum, London**
Codex Forster I, II and *III*
(c. 1487–1505)

◆ **Biblioteca Reale, Turin**
Codex on the Flight of Birds (1505)

◆ **Biblioteca Vaticana, Rome**
Codex Urbinas (c. 1530)

◆ **British Library**
Codex Arundel (1480–1518)

DRAWINGS

■ **British Museum, London**

■ **Royal Collection, Windsor**

■ **Metropolitan Museum of Art, New York**

■ **Musée du Louvre, Paris**

■ **Ashmolean Museum, Oxford**

■ **Uffizi Gallery, Florence**

■ **Biblioteca Reale, Turin**

■ **Galleria dell'Accademia, Venice**

■ **Szépmüvészeti Múzeum, Budapest**

■ **Museum Boijmans Van Beuningen, Rotterdam**

■ **National Gallery, London**

LEGACY

89

TYPOGRAPHIC LEONARDO

cartography

perspective

ideal city

The Deluge

Genius

Uccello

Invention

Leonardo

Milan

The Last Supper

Nature

parachute

military

Paintings

da Vinci

Engineering

microcosm

Sfumato

Giant horse

Anatomy

mirror writing

helicopter

Divine harmony

Codex Atlanticus

Notebooks

Florence

Vinci

Vitruvian Man

Drawing

Microcosm

Visionary

submarine

Virgin of the Rocks

Mona Lisa

Sculpture

Vortex

architecture

Renaissance man

Francesco Melzi

Treatise on Painting

Paragone

tank

Ludovico Sforza

Vitruvius

cannon

Observation

Michelangelo

dissection

flying machine

Codex Leicester

BIOGRAPHIES

Andrea del Verrocchio (c. 1435–88)
Florentine painter, sculptor and goldsmith who was Leonardo's teacher from about c. 1469. He was the master of one of the most important artistic workshops in Florence, through which a number of significant artists passed.

Ludovico Sforza (1452–1508)
Duke of Milan from 1494 until 1499, he was Leonardo's most significant single patron. He commissioned *The Last Supper* mural and the never-completed monument to his father, the Sforza horse.

Lisa Gherardini (1479–1542)
The model for Leonardo's most famous painting, she married Francesco del Giocondo, a well-off silk merchant, in 1495. She had five children and died in a convent in Florence, having never taken possession of her much-travelled portrait.

Lorenzo de' Medici (1449–92)
The de facto ruler of the Republic of Florence during Leonardo's youth, and a noted patron of the arts. Lorenzo may have been instrumental in sending Leonardo to Milan in 1481 as part of a diplomatic mission to Ludovico Sforza.

Michelangelo Buonarroti (1475–1564)
Sculptor, painter, architect and poet, Michelangelo was Leonardo's fiercest rival for the status of greatest living artist, though their personalities and outlook were polar opposites.

Raphael (1483–1520)
Along with Leonardo and Michelangelo, Raphael completed the trinity of High Renaissance masters, and his work shows the influence of Leonardo.

Luca Pacioli (c. 1447–1517)
A Franciscan friar and mathematician, who met Leonardo when he joined the court of Ludovico Sforza in 1497. Leonardo provided the illustrations for Pacioli's book *De Divina Proportione* (1509).

Giovanni Francesco Melzi (c. 1491–c. 1570)
The son of a Milanese nobleman, Melzi joined Leonardo's entourage in 1506 and became his companion. Melzi was Leonardo's executor, and produced a famous chalk portrait of Leonardo now in the Royal Collection at Windsor.

Francis I (1494–1547)
King of France from 1515 until his death, Francis was Leonardo's final patron from 1516. Leonardo brought a number of his paintings with him to the king's court, which remained in France after his death.

Giorgio Vasari (1511–74)
A painter, architect and writer, Vasari is best-known for his *Lives of the Most Excellent Painters, Sculptors and Architects*, first published in 1550. This was the main source of information about Leonardo up until the mid-19th century.

Giovanni Ambrogio de Predis (c. 1455–c. 1508)
Painter and miniaturist who collaborated with Leonardo, and with his brother, Evangelista, on the *Virgin of the Rocks* altarpiece. The brothers are credited with the side panels.

Isabella d'Este (1474–1539)
Marchioness of Mantua from 1490, Isabella was one of the most important patrons of the arts in Renaissance Italy. She commissioned a portrait from Leonardo, but only the cartoon was ever completed. She has been proposed as a potential model for the *Mona Lisa*.

● fellow artist ● patron
● model ● companion

INDEX

A

A Bear Walking 88
Adoration of the Magi 89
Al Biruni 84
anatomical drawings 9, 10,
  72–3
  Vitruvian Man 62–3
Annunciation, The 20, 55,
  89
appearance 22–3
Arconati, Marquis Galaezzo
  61

B

Baptism of Christ, The
  (Verrocchio) 54
Battle of Anghiari 30, 70,
  71, 76
Battle of Cascina
  (Michelangelo) 70, 71
Beauvoir, Simone de 85
Belle Ferronnière, La 89
Benois Madonna, The 89
bobbin-winder 83
Boltraffio, Giovanni 33
bombards 58
Book of the Courtier, The
  (Castiglione) 50
Borgia, Cesare 31, 45
Botticelli, Sandro 45
Bramante, Donato 45
bridges 58, 82
Brown, Dan; *The Da Vinci
  Code* 87

C

canal, scheme for 64–5
Caprotti, Gian Giacomo see
  Salaí
car 82
Castiglione, Baldassare:
  The Book of the Courtier
  50
catapults 59

chariots, covered 58
Charles II, governor of
  Milan 30
city states 38–41
clothes 22–3
Codex Atlanticus 60–1
Comfort, Alex 85
Compagnia di S. Luca,
  Florence 20
Confraternity of the
  Immaculate Conception
  21, 68, 69
crossbow 83

D

Da Vinci Code, The (Brown)
  87
Dante 80
Darwin, Charles 42, 43
death 31, 34
diving suit 83

Dufy, Raoul 24
Dürer, Albrecht 24

E

Empedocles 26
equestrian monument 21,
  66–7
Escher, M.C. 24

F

family tree 18–19
flight 56–7
Florence 14, 16, 20, 30, 31,
  39, 40, 70
Francesco di Antonio da
  Vinci 18, 19
Francis I, of France 30, 34,
  93
Frederick III, Holy Roman
  Emperor 17
Fry, C. B. 85

G

Galileo 84
Gherardini, Lisa 30, 80, 92
Ghiberti, Lorenzo 16
Ghirlandaio, Domenico 44
Giocondo, Francesco del
  30, 80
Giorgio, Francesco di 45
Giorgio Martini, Francesco
  di 93
gliders 56–7, 83
Gogh, Vincent van 25
guns 59

H

Hamilton, Gavin 69
hang glider 83
helicopter design 56, 83
herb sauce 27
Hildegard of Bingen 84
Holbein, Hans, the Younger
  24
homosexuality 20, 33
horse, giant sculpture 21,
  66–7

I

inventions
  did they work? 82–3
  flight 56–7
  military 58–9
  scheme for canal 64–5
Italian city states 38–9

J

Julius II, Pope 70

K

Klee, Paul 24

L

Lady with an Ermine 89
Last Supper, The 21, 74–5,
  76, 89

Leda and the Swan 49, 76
Leden, Judy 57
left-handedness 24–5
lens grinder 82
Leoni, Pompeo 60, 61
library, Leonardo's 28–9
Linnaeus, Carl 43
lion, mechanical 31
Lippi, Filippino 44
locations of works 88–9
Los Alporchones, Battle of (1452) 16
lost works 76
Louis XII, of France 21

M
Machiavelli, Niccolò 36, 40, 45
Madonna of the Carnation, The 89
Madonna of the Yarnwinder 89
Medici, Giuliano de' 31
Medici, Lorenzo de' 40, 92
Medici, Lorenzo di Piero de' 31
Meijer, Frederik 67
Melzi, Giovanni Francesco 32, 34, 60, 61, 93
Michelangelo Buonarroti 8, 14, 44, 92
Battle of Cascina 70, 71
rivalry with Leonardo 46–7
Milan 20, 21, 30, 31, 39, 40, 41, 58
military inventions 58–9
Mona Lisa 30, 80–1, 89
adaptations of 86–7
Monet, Claude 25
Munch, Edvard 25

N
Napoleon Bonaparte 60
notebooks 10, 26, 32, 34, 89
Codex Atlanticus 60–1

O
Oggiono, Marco d' 33

P
Pacioli, Luca 31, 39, 45, 93
parachute 82
paragone 50
Picasso, Pablo 25, 81
Plotinus 26
Pollaiuolo, Antonio 44
Porphyry of Tyre 26
Portrait of a Musician 89
Portrait of Ginevra de' Benci 89
Predis, Giovanni Ambrogio de 93
Pythagoras 26

R
rack & pinion 83
Raphael 24, 45, 92
Rembrandt 25
'Renaissance man' 84–5
Richard III, of England 17
Rubens, Peter Paul 24
Battle of Anghiari (copy after Leonardo) 71

S
St. Jerome 88, 89
St. John the Baptist 89
Salaí (Gian Giacomo Caprotti) 31, 32, 34
Sangallo, *Aristotele da: Battle of Cascina* (copy after Michelangelo) 70
Savonarola, Girolamo 40
Sforza, Francesco 41

equestrian monument 21, 66–7
Sforza, Ludovico 16, 20, 21, 31, 41, 58, 66, 69, 92
Sforza Castle, Milan: *Sala delle Asse* 76
sfumato 55, 80
'Squaring the Circle' 62
Study of a Deluge 49
swing bridge 82

T
Taine, Hippolyte 79
tank 82
Toulouse-Lautrec, Henri de 24
travels 30–1
tunnelling, methods of 58

V
Vasari, Giorgio 8, 44, 75, 76, 93
vegetarianism 26–7
Venice 31, 39
Verrocchio, Andrea del 20, 44, 92
The Baptism of Christ 54
Vinci, Antonio da 18, 19
Vinci, Ser Piero da 14
Virgin and Child with St Anne, The 88, 89
Virgin of the Rocks 21, 68–9, 89
Vitruvian Man 62–3
vortices 48–9

W
water 48, 49
weapons 21, 58–9
Welles, Orson 85
world in 1452 16–17
worm gear 83

ACKNOWLEDGMENTS

Picture credits
The publishers would like to thank the following for permission to reproduce their images in this book. Every effort has been made to acknowledge copyright holders, and the publishers apologize for any omissions.

7 © Shutterstock.
14 © Shutterstock/Everett Historical.
15 © Shutterstock/Schwabenblitz.
20 © Dover Images.
21 © Dover Images.
46 © Shutterstock/Angela Jones.
47 © Dover Images.
48 © Getty Images/Corbis Fine Art.
49 © Shutterstock.
49 © Shutterstock/Angela Jones.
54 © FineArt / Alamy Stock Photo.
55 © Dover Images.
60 © Dover Images.

63 © Shutterstock/ARCHITECTEUR.
65 © Getty Images/Apic.
68 © Dover Images.
69 © Dover Images.
70 © Getty Images/De Agostini Picture Library.
71 © University of Leuven.
73 © Shutterstock/bluezace.
74 © Dover Images.
80 © Shutterstock.
81 © Shutterstock.
88 © Dover Images.